MANY

MOTHERS,

SEVEN

SKIES

SCENES FOR TOMORROW

Many Mothers, Seven Skies

JOAN CRATE • CHERYL FOGGO • TCHITALA NYOTA KAMBA
SHERRY LETENDRE • KAREN W. OLSON • SUSAN OURIOU
in consultation and conversation with LINDA GABORIAU

Canada Council for the Arts   Conseil des Arts du Canada   Alberta Government   Canada   calgaryarts development

Many thanks to the Canada Council for the Arts and the Calgary Arts Development Authority for providing the grants that made our collective's dream a reality. Freehand Books also acknowledges the financial support for its publishing program provided by the Canada Council for the Arts and the Alberta Media Fund, and by the Government of Canada through the Canada Book Fund.

Freehand Books
515–815 1st Street sw   Calgary, Alberta   T2P 1N3
www.freehand-books.com

Book orders: UTP Distribution
5201 Dufferin Street   Toronto, Ontario   M3H 5T8
Telephone: 1-800-565-9523 Fax: 1-800-221-9985
utpbooks@utpress.utoronto.ca   utpdistribution.com

Library and Archives Canada Cataloguing in Publication
Title: Many mothers, seven skies : scenes for tomorrow / Joan Crate, Cheryl Foggo, Tchitala Nyota Kamba, Sherry Letendre, Karen W. Olson, Susan Ouriou ; in consultation and conversation with Linda Gaboriau.
Names: Crate, Joan, 1953– author. | Foggo, Cheryl, author. | Olson, Karen W., 1957– author. | Gaboriau, Linda, contributor.
Identifiers: Canadiana (print) 20230453988 | Canadiana (ebook) 20230458157 | ISBN 9781990601521 (softcover) | ISBN 9781990601545 (PDF) | ISBN 9781990601538 (EPUB)
Subjects: LCSH: Canadian drama—21st century. | LCSH: Canadian drama—Women authors. | CSH: Canadian drama (English)—21st century | CSH: Canadian drama (English)—Women authors.
Classification: LCC PS8315.1 .M36 2023 | DDC c812/.60809287—dc23

Book design by Natalie Olsen
Back cover image: beadwork by the Many Mothers Collective
Printed on FSC® recycled paper and bound in Canada by Imprimerie Gauvin

CONTENTS

ABOUT THE MANY MOTHERS

INTRODUCTION

Susan Ouriou brought us together.

My husband, a Lebanese Canadian, was dying, and Tchi-tala Nyota Kamba, a French-speaking immigrant from the Democratic Republic of the Congo, had been widowed not long before our collective began. Sue knew loss, too, her daughter Katie having died at just sixteen years old. We were women bereaved, but not just by death. We were worried about our planet and what the future would hold for the generations to come. Mothers and grandmothers, we needed hope. We wanted to do something.

Sue brought us together.

Sherry Letendre from the Alexis Nakota Sioux Nation is an intergenerational survivor of the residential school system who Sue met at the Truth and Reconciliation Commission. Sherry worked in the Nakota interpretation booth and Sue in the French booth. Mentoring youth in her community, Sherry weaves traditional teachings into contemporary lives. We welcomed her.

Karen W. Olson was director of the Indigenous Emerging Writers residency at the Banff Centre when Sue, working as interpreter and translator in English and French, met her. Originally from the Peguis Nation (Ininiwak/Anishinaabe) in Manitoba, Karen now lives in Penticton and teaches creative writing at the En'owkin Centre on the traditional and unceded territory of the Syilx Okanagan people. She joined our circle.

Cheryl Foggo, a playwright, filmmaker and author, lives on the traditional territories of the Niitsitapi (Blackfoot Confederacy), Tsuu T'ina and Stoney Nakoda, and Region 3 of the Métis Nation. Although her Black foremothers and fathers made Alberta their home well over a century ago, her family members — like countless other Black Canadians — still hear jeers of, "Why don't you go back to where you came from?" We welcomed Cheryl in, too.

Sue met literary translator Linda Gaboriau, our theatre consultant, at the Banff Centre, where they were co-founders of the Banff International Literary Translation Centre (BILTC). Under Linda's directorship, the residency was described (by a participant, and later faculty member) as an international asylum for the sane in a world gone mad. Linda became the newest member of the group we began to call *Many Mothers*. She is based in Tiohtià:ke, now known as Montreal, and divides her time between there and her family home within the ancestral territory of the Wampanoag in Massachusetts.

Both Sue and I, like Tchitala and Cheryl, are based in Mohkinstsis — or Calgary — which became our meeting place.

The seven of us, a diverse group of elders, have endured, loved, lost and celebrated life in our own ways. Now, we decided, we would write a production for the stage, voicing our different experiences and what we came to realize are similar concerns about the future of our families, our planet, its peoples and its incredible network of flora and fauna.

Instead of arriving with scenes in hand, we began by talking and getting to know one another. We came together in October 2020, able to take advantage of a small window in time, despite COVID. The out-of-towners slept in Sue's home, and we gathered in a circle all day for a week in a community hall. Every morning, one member would open with a prayer: Karen with sweetgrass from her Peguis tradition, Sherry (participating via Zoom) with sage from her Alexis Nakota Sioux Nation, Tchitala ringing a cowbell from her African village to call on the ancestors to accompany us. Some of our planned activities were altered or cancelled due to the pandemic, but mid-week, we visited the Tsuu T'ina museum in the morning and learned from our guide the long history of this area. That afternoon, Cheryl guided us through Heritage Park sites with relevance to Black history in southern Alberta. Cheryl works with the Park to have Black history formally acknowledged onsite.

Mentors such as Jenna Rodgers, then-Director of Chromatic Theatre, Michelle Thrush, Artistic Director of Making Treaty 7, and Reneltta Arluk, then-Director of Indigenous Arts at the Banff Centre shared their knowledge with us. Throughout the week, we listened to each other's worlds, shared meals, wrote, beaded, drummed, sang, laughed and cried.

We returned to our home bases to work, checking in every few months via Zoom. For our next in-person week, held in June 2021, we brought in actors and a director to work with us. Their talents and insights were invaluable and we thank them for making our two-dimensional scripts fill out and breathe: director Michelle Thrush and actors Elizabeth Breaker, Andy Curtis, Stacy Da Silva, Ivanna Ihekwoaba,

Norma Lewis, Allison Lynch, and Chantal Perron. Some of the same actors came together in October 2021 for the fine-tuning of our scenes as well as Reneltta Arluk, Wakefield Brewster, Janelle Cooper, Douglas MacLeod and singer Barbara Joan Scott. Thanks also to Barb for her watchful eyes and suggestions on our scripts as they developed.

Throughout our two-year process, some of our circle could not always be with the rest of the Mothers in person due to illness, sometimes due to tragedy. During our time together, Sherry lost her grandson and mother and Karen also lost her mother. Like the earth, we sustain damage. We carry on.

The scenes that resulted from our process are as diverse as our collective, each one representing a glance at the world through different eyes, an alternate perspective, the focus shifting and changing from scene to scene. These scenes – standing shoulder to shoulder, each emphasizing the other through its very contrast – perhaps make the strongest statement of all. We are elders of various cultures who are concerned. We are women who appreciate and respect each other. We work together, and by doing that, have found our similarities within our differences – neither prescribed nor imposed – but implicit.

We believe the many peoples of the world can do the same. Let's heal our Mother Earth. Let's make it humanity's priority. Let's each do it in our own ways. Let's work together.

Thank you, Ishnish, Miigwech, Kininaskomitin, Aksanti, Tuasakidila, Merci.

Joan Crate

After Winter

Joan Crate

ARTIST'S STATEMENT

The past seven decades of prime-time newscasts are potent history lessons. I'm interested in the way television news both reflects and affects Canadian society. While documenting major events, newscasters influence how men and women dress, groom, behave and relate to each other. It's against the backdrop of major news stories that we live our lives.

In the past decade, the way the news is regarded has changed significantly. While the public came to accept the existence of bias along with their daily dose of information, the use of algorithms now creates different "realities" for different groups, while phrases such as "post-truth" and "alternate facts" emphasize our lack of commonality in an increasingly troubled world. In "And Now for the News," the mogul's voice is a reminder that the truth and substance of a story are treated as less important than the attention the story can generate.

While the news scene is meant to be little more than a summary of recent history, I hope it also demonstrates that there are always those who will speak up against persons and systems trying to conceal inopportune facts from the public.

My first scene in the anthology, "After Winter," is much more personal, dealing with the death of my partner of thirty-eight years at the beginning of the pandemic. Like so many others, I found solace in the natural world. Under the stars and within the sand and rock of my Okanagan "garden," I rediscovered the intricate web of life, death, scale, time and infinity; there is no other way to put it. In confronting one of life's most tragic and common events, I attempt to give death – if not meaning – at least a context.

In both scenes I use a plant – a living, growing entity – as a symbol of hope being delivered to the future.

CHARACTERS
Woman
Man

SETTING
House and garden

*Upstage: a bedroom with a woman under the covers, a man
on top of the covers. Downstage, a counter with a can of coffee,
a coffee maker, two cups, a microwave, and a bottle of liquor
in the cupboard below or above it. Also, a small kitchen table
with two chairs. On the back of a chair, a housecoat or shawl.
Unlit downstage left or right is a garden scene.*

WOMAN wakes up in bed. Sits up.

WOMAN: Morning, lovely man. How are you feeling?

Waits.

WOMAN: Hey, are you warm enough?

*Strokes the side of his face. Pulls a blanket over him, kisses
him.*

My poor sick guy.

*She takes his pulse. Nods slowly. She gets up, goes to the
table, pours half a cup of coffee and puts it in the microwave.
While the coffee heats up, she looks out the window.*

(*Sarcastically*) Oh good, another spring snowfall!

*Hugs herself, retrieves the coffee from the microwave, goes to
the cupboard, pulls out a bottle of liquor and pours it in until
the cup is full.*

It's cold in here.

Takes a swig.

Why is it so damn cold?

(*Calling over to* MAN *on bed*) Remember how hot it was last summer at the cabin? And all those deer coming down the hill early in the morning, wanting to eat our tomatoes? So many damn deer, but majestic. You said a lot of them would be shot once hunting season opened in the fall. Then there's the natural predators. Wolves and cougars. A pack of coyotes can disrupt a herd, pick off some of the fawns, you said. The does can't get to them, just have to watch their young being murdered.

> *Glances over at the bed, then turns back to the window and takes a drink.*

I don't know how you watch something like that.

And the deer hit on roads. How many was it we saw last year? At least three.

> *Drinks more.*

The damn crows swoop in, pecking and pulling, guts hanging from their beaks.

> *Shudders. Pours more liquor in her cup and drinks.*

Finally the bones, some still with hair and skin. Scattered by predators. Hey, remember that deer leg the dog got? We just let her chew it until there was nothing left.

> *Drinks.*

It's easier to contend with in the summer. Death. Disappearance.

> *Lights down on the bed.* WOMAN *sits at the table with her coffee/whiskey mix.*

Those long summer days that stretch out and make you think they'll last forever.

Lights fading into a brilliant sunset, slowly going down to evening semi-darkness as she speaks.

You don't even notice day is ending until you see the first blush of sunset. Then blazes of scarlet and orange, so bright, the colours mesmerize you right into nightfall.

MAN comes in with a tray, a cocktail for himself and a plate of cheese, crackers and grapes for both.

MAN kisses WOMAN's head as he sets down the plate and his drink. Stars start to come out in the sky. He puts his hand on her shoulder and points with the other.

MAN: Look over there. Jupiter's just starting to show. And there, that's Mars.

WOMAN smiles, touches his hand on her shoulder.

WOMAN: Yes, creeping over Jupiter's shoulder.

Turns slightly.

That glow on the horizon must be the Milky Way.

MAN sits and WOMAN adjusts her seat to look at the Milky Way. MAN does the same.

MAN: Stars so far away in space and time, they're just a blur of light.

WOMAN: The Wolf Trail. Where the dead go, some say. The Spirit Path.

MAN: Molecules in infinity.

WOMAN looks around the sky.

WOMAN: It all makes me feel like I'm… I'm…

MAN: (*finishes her sentence, slightly breathless*) part of something much greater.

WOMAN: (*laughs*) I was going to say completely inconsequential.

Both laugh.

Light fades. MAN rises, takes her hand, kisses it, but as she gets up for a hug, he quickly exits. Confused, she sits back down. Lights back up on WOMAN sitting at her table in the kitchen with her cup of whiskey/coffee just as she was.

WOMAN grabs a housecoat from the back of his chair, rises, wraps it around herself, rubs her arms.

WOMAN: It's freezing in here.

Checks the window to make sure it's closed. Hand over the heat vent.

The heat's coming through, but the cold… like an Arctic front. It just… swallows… everything.

Hugs self and calls out.

Why is it so damn cold in this house?

Two people in colourless clothing come from offside. She follows to watch them go to the bed, wrap MAN's body in sheets and take it away.

Fade out, then the spotlight comes up on WOMAN.

WOMAN: (*shocked, moves awkwardly back to the kitchen*) You are ashes and memory now, a sealed marble urn.

Puts her hand on the coffee can, which is looking urn-like in the light. WOMAN picks up the cup, tries to pour a cup of coffee, but her hand shakes, puts it down. Speaks to the can.

We're in quarantine together, oh God, your charred remains and my scattered grey thoughts.

Pauses, shakes her head.

Alexa, turn on the news.

Sfx of COVID news, just audible but not clear.

RADIO: … three more dead and three hundred and fifteen new cases in the city. Canada has reached 1,000 COVID deaths and numbers are rising…

WOMAN: Alexa, shut up! Is there nothing but the damn pandemic?

No weather, no accidents?

Pauses, trying to remember.

Last night I'm sure I heard brakes squeal and metal crunch. Now (*looks down at her legs, then at her hands*) I have road rash down my legs and glass imbedded in my palms (*sfx of a police siren starts up, climaxing with her very loud scream*). Screaming like a siren.

Screams into her hands.

Fade out as WOMAN takes off her housecoat, puts on a straw hat, gardening gloves, picks up the coffee can. As lights come up, sunny yellow, sfx birds chirping, WOMAN moves into the garden area — flowers and other plants, soil, etc.

I go to ground. Like you, I go to the earth that is made of loss itself.

Kneels or bends down, picks up a trowel and starts to dig.

The oil, water and minerals it gives up, its pillage by flood and drought.

Opens the coffee can.

The dead it buries.

Scoops ashes into the soil.

Pokes through the soil with her hands.

Spiders' eggs. Oh!

Pulls back.

A wasps' nest. Is that a snail?

Picks up the shell, then replaces it.

Yes, tucked in a crevice. All these tiny lives. Within all this microscopic life. Within a universe.

WOMAN scoops more ashes and some soil into a plant pot, puts in a plant and carries it into the next scene.

(*Exiting*) We all want our lives to mean something.

END

And Now for the News

Joan Crate

CHARACTERS
News channel mogul (voice-over)
Kent Clarke – newscaster
Norma Jean Monroe – newscaster

SETTING
A television newsroom

*A CBV TV logo is behind newscasters who are seated at a desk.
It remains there when no other photos or videos are in the
background. News clips must go quickly from one newscaster
to the other, incorporating lighting changes and sound effects
seamlessly.*

*As the newscast goes from the '50s to present times, screens
with visuals to match the stories play behind the newscasters,
first just the logo, then black and white photos, finally going to
video as technology changes.*

*The actors will change hairstyles, wigs and accessories — in
keeping with changing fashion — between announcements.
The lighting design will evolve as the male and female newscasters achieve a more equal status.*

NEWS CHANNEL MOGUL'S VOICE: *(voice deep, God-like)* Citizens of
the Dominion of Canada,

Lights start to slowly come up on the '50s style newsroom.

we bring you attractive newscasters with important stories
direct from our team of investigative reporters. And now
for *(drum roll)* THE NEWS.

*An actor brings in a plant from the previous scene and places
it on NORMA JEAN's desk. NORMA JEAN, in a blonde wig, is
looking in a compact and putting on a sweep of red lipstick.*

KENT: *(authoritative voice)* This is Kent Clarke

NORMA JEAN: *(chirpily)* and Norma Jean Monroe

KENT: with a man's

NORMA JEAN: and a gal's

KENT: perspective on the news.

KENT: This just in, North Korea has invaded South Korea.

NORMA JEAN: (*"cutesy" and vying for Kent's attention, which she does not get*) The Diner's Club is introducing something called a "credit card." Not sure what that is, Kent, but ladies, let's hope it encourages our hubbies to take us out to dinner.

KENT: The United States begins the development of the hydrogen bomb. Renowned physicist Albert Einstein warns the world that a nuclear war would lead to mutual destruction.

> *KENT puts on a thin moustache.*

NORMA JEAN: Golly, Kent, there's a new craze and it's called the Twist.

NEWS CHANNEL MOGUL'S VOICE: (*Both NORMA JEAN and KENT look up, startled, as he begins to speak.*) Norma Jean, let's see some action. Up. (*NORMA JEAN rises.*) Dance.

NORMA JEAN: (*starts dancing tentatively, then gets into it*) Chubby Checker danced the Twist while singing his song on *The Dick Clark Show.* Now everyone's doing it!

> *Lights go down before NORMA JEAN has finished. Awkwardly, she sits in the brief black/brownout.*

> *A paper is dropped on KENT's desk. He picks it up, glances at it and positions himself as far away from NORMA JEAN as possible.*

KENT: President Kennedy has been assassinated in Dallas, Texas. Shots rang out as he, Mrs. Kennedy and the Governor drove in an open limousine. Mrs. Kennedy was heard to cry out "Oh no!"

NORMA JEAN: Oh no!

KENT: (*completely ignores her, but is uncharacteristically shaken*)
as the president slumped in her arms.

NORMA JEAN: It looks like the hippies are joining the scientists,
uh, Kent. Canadian scientist Dr. Donald Chant is attracting
followers to protest such issues as air pollution, water pollution, hazardous waste and the careless use of pesticides.

NORMA JEAN changes blonde wig to long straight hair.

KENT: President Johnson has increased the number of troops
sent to South Vietnam to over half a million. Bombs, artillery,
napalm and Agent Orange are just some of the weapons to
be used on the Vietnamese.

*KENT combs hair from slicked back to longish Beatle-ish style
and exchanges thin tie for more flamboyant one.*

NORMA JEAN: Draft-dodgers and deserters are flooding into
Canada. Approximately 125,000 are expected to cross the
border.

NORMA JEAN adds granny glasses à la Gloria Steinem.

A paper is dropped on KENT's desk. KENT picks it up and reads it.

KENT: Martin Luther King Jr. has been assassinated in
Memphis, Tennessee. King, a non-violent protest advocate
and leader in the civil rights movement, was a target of
J. Edgar Hoover and the FBI who attempted to discredit
him and the movement right up to his murder.

NORMA JEAN: Oh n—

NEWS CHANNEL MOGUL'S VOICE: (*cuts in*) Norma Jean! Look,
we're going to give you a few important stories, but don't get

emotional. And don't think you can get equal pay… EVER.

NORMA JEAN: Oh— (*turns abruptly to another camera and from here on is as uninvolved as Kent in the news stories and more "professional"*) The United States has put a man on the moon. By the 21st century, various nations will have left almost 190,000 kilograms of cast-off material.

KENT: Police arrested burglars in the Democratic National Committee headquarters at the Watergate complex in Washington, D.C. Nixon and his aides instructed the CIA to impede the FBI's investigation of the crime.

NORMA JEAN: In what has been termed the "Battle of the Sexes" tennis match, the female tennis player Billie Jean King beats male tennis player Bobby Riggs.

> *NORMA JEAN goes back to the short blonde wig and a jacket with huge shoulder pads.*

> *KENT starts to acknowledge NORMA JEAN's existence, at first with glances in her direction and later with interaction.*

KENT: We have an AIDS epidemic. Some religious leaders are calling AIDS the Gay Plague as tens of thousands die in Canada, hundreds of thousands in the United States, and millions around the world. Of both sexes.

NORMA JEAN: Development of the Alberta Oil Sands is bringing Alberta a thriving economy and Canada's fastest growing source of greenhouse gas emissions, which scientists warn will cause global warming and lead to devastating Climate Change.

> *NORMA JEAN takes off the jacket with huge shoulder pads.*

> *A paper is dropped on KENT's desk.*

KENT: No such thing, Norma Jean. (*picks up paper and reads*) But as we enter the new century, known as Y2K, all computers will crash, causing a worldwide standstill.

NORMA JEAN: No such thing, Ke—

NEWS CHANNEL MOGUL'S VOICE: (*God-like, slight reverberation*) Now a few words from our sponsor. As General Motors go, so goes the entire North American economy, Norma Jean.

NORMA JEAN: N.J. Please call me N.J. (*then quickly carries on*) Pro-democracy protests take place at Tiananmen Square, China.

N.J. ties a "pussy bow" around her neck.

KENT: The Exxon Valdez oil tanker spill contaminates nearly two thousand kilometres of shoreline in British Columbia and Alaska.

KENT goes back to the thin tie and tousled hair.

N.J.: The Berlin Wall falls.

KENT: We have some footage of the Gulf War that looks like a… video game?

NEWS CHANNEL MOGUL'S VOICE: A new strategy, Kent and N.J. We're going to cover stories in two-second sound bites for the millennials. Let's go!

KENT and N.J. exchange a quick look, swipe papers from the desk and stare ahead as if at a video prompter, talking quickly as images behind them change.

N.J.: Nine Eleven

N.J. yanks "pussy bow" from around her neck.

KENT: The invasion of Afghanistan

N.J.: Increasing cancer and respiratory illnesses

KENT: The invasion of Iraq

N.J.: Tornadoes, floods, drought, earthquakes

KENT: School shootings, murders of Black males by police, missing and murdered Indigenous women and girls

N.J.: Fewer fish, bats, song birds. One thousand species a year decimated

KENT: And the pandemic. (*sticks finger in ear to simulate an earphone*) This from a news feed: COVID escaped from a Chinese lab. (*sticks finger in other ear to simulate another earphone*) No. The pandemic is a hoax!

N.J.: Science doesn't support that, Kent. Millions around the world have died from COVID-19 and are still dying.

KENT: Hospitals are overcrowded, health care in crisis and there's increasing polarization among the public.

> *KENT unbuttons his shirt and loosens his tie.*

N.J.: Meanwhile, hundreds of bodies of Indigenous children are being found in unmarked graves near residential schools across Canada.

> *N.J. puts hand over her mouth, smudging her lipstick.*

KENT: (*exhausted*) The Taliban have taken over Afghanistan.

N.J.: Russia has invaded Ukraine.

> *N.J. looks at KENT, worried.*

KENT: World leaders fear a nuclear Armageddon.

KENT looks back at N.J., both horrified.

NEWS CHANNEL MOGUL'S VOICE: Stop, stop. No one wants bad news all the time. We're introducing dancing cats and quirky dogs.

On the screen behind them, shots of adorable/cute/funny animals while KENT and N.J. register shock. Behind this, the sound of the NEWS CHANNEL MOGUL laughing at the antics on screen.

Look at that. Awww, cute.

KENT: This isn't actually news.

N.J.: What happened to investigative journalism?

NEWS CHANNEL MOGUL'S VOICE: Look, people believe what they want, despite the facts. No one takes the news seriously anymore.

N.J.: Maybe we should go somewhere they do, Kent.

N.J. picks up the plant from her desk and holds it protectively as she and KENT stand.

NEWS CHANNEL MOGUL'S VOICE: Fine. I don't need you.

N.J. and KENT storm off-stage.

NEWS CHANNEL MOGUL'S VOICE: Get back here. (*wheedling*) I won't even make you dye your hair.

END

The
Sender

Cheryl Foggo

ARTIST'S STATEMENT

Some years ago a friend in the Mohkinstsis arts community said, "The real currency of this life is the people you meet through the work." In this regard, I have been amply rewarded by my time spent with the women of this collective. We taught and we learned.

During the process, I wrote a scene called "The Promise" about my beloved sister's death. We all liked the scene and it blended well with the other works in this anthology. As the time to publish and stage the project drew closer, however, I could no longer bear to witness and revisit the loss of Noël through the piece I had written.

Susan generously asked me to contribute something else, the collective lovingly agreed, and Susan suggested the scene you find here, "The Sender," which she had viewed on CBC Gem in 2021.

I wrote "The Sender" for Obsidian Theatre Company's 21 Black Futures project. Among the few stipulations placed on subject matter for the twenty-one writers on that assignment was that the pieces had to be set in the future. In my playwright's notes for the production I described it this way:

In my vision of the future where "The Sender" is set, a global project to eliminate racism and its associated effects has resulted in a world that is peaceful, logical and sustainable.

I would like to thank Leah Simone-Bowen for her intelligent direction and Amanda Cordner for her brilliant performance as Cil in the original production of this short play.

Although I didn't write "The Sender" for the Many Mothers Collective, conversations I had in the rooms we shared impacted my thinking during its creation.

Those conversations that unfolded as we snacked, laughed, listened to each other and the actors read, listened to music, beaded, shared sacred practices, went on field trips and washed our coffee cups at the end of the day also greatly influenced my writing of "The Promise," and perhaps someday I will find the strength to return to the memories of my sister that are held there.

Regardless, I will always cherish the richness of the kinship I found with Joan, Karen, Linda, Sherry, Sue and Tchitala.

INT. OFFICE SPACE - DAY

CIL is seated at her monitor. There is a large, raised red button at her desk, clearly visible.

She stretches, the end of a long work day. A pleasant TONE sounds, indicating her System has logged in.

She touches a device in her ear.

CIL: Hey System.

Yep, pretty straightforward. The couple that ran the Rights for Whites website tried to smuggle a bunch of music.

Ya, no doubt.

Other than that smooth as glass. Oh, except I had one weird glitch a couple hours ago.

Like a power surge or something. Maybe ask maintenance to schedule a scan of my LX tonight.

So just one more for today right?

Do I have his data?

A SOUND indicates a file's been uploaded to her monitor. She gives it a quick scan.

Got it. He's Implicit Consent with a Code 3 Complaint.

Go ahead and upsync us. Talk to you later.

A SOUND indicates System's departure.

Good afternoon, 26-year-old Terrance Knight.

This is Transport Room 5.

Mr. Knight, I understand you have lodged a complaint relating to the diagnosis of cataracts in your left eye prior to signing the terms that will enable your transfer to White Supremacist Island.

The Board of Compassionate Exemptions and Extensions has reviewed and denied your complaint.

No.

That has nothing to do with me. Completely different department.

Now I can assure you, cataract surgery is available on White Supremacist Island.

True, the procedure that utilizes the Laserphaco Probe will not be avail…

Not negotiable.

If you would…

It's…

She lifts a hand and raises her voice.

Mr. Knight!

I am authorized to offer advice at my discretion, therefore I will take a moment to point out that your attempt to shout over my communication is a symptom of your chronic interrupting and multi-splaining. This behaviour is even unpopular on White Supremacist Island and there are a lot of quick-tempered people over there. Consider yourself warned.

The Laserphaco Probe is subject to statute 43.

Residents of White Supremacist Island forfeit all inventions, improvements and popular entertainments that can be directly linked to Indigenous, Black or Persons of Colour. The Laserphaco Probe is a patented invention by Patricia Bath, a Black woman.

You'll get the other cataract surgery once you get over there and it'll probably be fine. Plus, look at everything else you're getting! No, I know you haven't signed yet, but just hypothetically.

The luxury high-rise includes built-in gaming wall, ion-factor surround sound and dishwasher. Since you're not a voluntary you can't have the three bedroom, but I'll get you two plus den with a bath and a half. There's an infinity pool and virtual forest sauna on the 22nd floor.

Well sure, there's always fine print.

The elevators are not equipped with the automatic closing doors that include the flexible belt improvement patented by Alexander Miles, a Black man. This does mean there is increased risk of falling down the elevator shaft, so getting up to the pool is… Well. The staircases are safe!

The island has a temperate climate. There are jobs. The beaches are…

Her station glitches. The lights dim briefly. We hear a
POWERFUL RUSH OF WATER, a WHOOSHING SOUND. When the
lights come back up, a few CONSOLE LIGHTS are FLASHING.

CIL: *(to herself)* What's happening?

Mr. Knight! Are you still there?

CIL presses her ear device, attempting to summon System 11-14.

System! System 11-14!

What's going on?

She's on her feet now. She repeatedly taps the device in her ear.

System 11-14 this is Cil.

This is Cil in Sending Room 5. Are you there? I'm having
an issue!

She presses the ear device again.

CIL: *(confused)* Who is this?

A long beat as she squints at her monitor and strains to hear.

Who?

Brittany who? Bree?

Bree Corbett!?

CIL drops into her chair, leans forward to get a better look.
She taps her ear device again.

System 11-14 I've been hacked! Subject Terrance Knight's briefing was aborted before he could sign and he's been transported. I'm requesting a retrieval for signature.

Bree shutup! I'm trying to get my…

She's still trying to get her System back.

What?

You got his signature? How? What are you…?

I can hardly hear you. My CPU is really unstable. Just a sec.

Okay that's better. Why do you have my transfer's signature and why are you here?! How did you…

Terrance Knight is Terry Thane?

Oh my God. Don't tell me you're still seeing Terry Thane.

How did you get him past my System? I'm not supposed to process files of people I know. A name change shouldn't have fooled it.

Wow. You're still as brilliant as ever I see. Stupidest smart person I've ever known.

I didn't recognize him at all. He looks terrible. Okay, give me the signature. Put it up on the Driver Glide and I can scan it to the…

She glances at her timer.

But I don't have time! My shift ends in fifteen minutes and if I don't have it in by end of day it doesn't count!

Which you well know from when you worked in Tech and Design!

You'll get me two signatures in exchange for a favour? Who's the other signature? Terry was my last file of the day.

What? Why? I thought you still had six months to go in rehab.

She brings up Bree's file.

I've got your file up here and... Dang. Terrible.

Out of the ten precepts of Racism Elimination 101 your scores are dismal on three of them.

Precept Two – Defending the words or actions of racists by saying "I'm sure they didn't mean it that way."

Five – Telling a racialized friend about a racist thing someone said behind their back but refusing to name the perp.

Seven – Expecting your racialized friends to tolerate your racist partner.

Oof, obviously still doing that.

Okay, this is bad but you've got six months to pull up your scores. Do you really want to spend the rest of your life on White Supremacist Island with him?

All right. Well, that's your choice. You know transfer is binding right?

You can never come back.

What are the perks you're looking for? No promises, but if I can get them for you I will.

You're 100% on this? You know that the end of sustainable life over there is outside our jurisdiction?

I don't know, I'm just. I guess I hoped for better, from you and for you.

Bree. Girl.

Remember when Terry was working at Lineco? And Asif got the promotion Terry thought he should have had? Remember how angry he was when he came over to your place? Ya, we were in the middle of a Janelle Monae dance party.

Anyway, Terry was looking for affirmation and you told him Asif seemed pretty brilliant?

Ya. He punched a hole in the wall. Does he still pull shit like that?

I know it's none of my business.

I'm only saying that just because he's not going to have Brown folks to blame for all his problems over there doesn't mean he's going to stop punching holes in walls.

Shrugs in surrender, looks at her timer.

Okay, we don't have much time, what do you want?

She types out Bree's list.

Uh huh. Right. What colour?

For how long? Okay, it's yours.

That'll be tough, those options are usually reserved for voluntaries. Although, I guess you're technically a voluntary, even though you hacked my station. Fine, I think I can get that.

What else?

Nope, that I cannot do. Cool Sports Network is not possible.

Because it includes Basketball, Football, Soccer, Track and Field and all the other sports that are dependent on majority labour of Black or Brown people. Statute Six, you've read the agreement. I can give you Relaxation Romps Network. It's got a bunch of stuff – curling, lawn bowling, darts, poker, it's still got the NHL, for now. That's the best I can do.

Is that everything?

She taps in some buttons on her screen, we hear a SEND sound.

Done.

All right, load those signatures.

*We hear a SOUND and two pages drop into CIL's hands.
She reads them.*

She looks at Bree.

Very funny Bree. Signed "What's her name" and "Who's-it."

All right. One down, one to go.

Brace yourself. It doesn't hurt but it's cold and wet.

Just what I said. One down – Terry Thane, also known as Terrance Knight. One to go – Brittany Corbett, also known as: My former friend.

I don't need your signature, you gave verbal consent. Verbal and Implicit are now valid. I mean we always want signature where possible, but it's not a requirement anymore. Think of signatures like trophies.

No, he really is gone Bree. Permanently.

Dead serious. You're actually the one that hit send when you hacked in, which is unfortunate because I find it deeply satisfying to punt the Terries.

Stop it. Oh for… there's a box of tissues behind you.

I wouldn't even if I could.

Well look at it from my perspective.

A PLEASANT TONE indicates CIL's System has checked in.

Hey System 11-14. No, I'm okay. Thanks for asking. It's fine, don't worry. See you tomorrow.

System tones out. Without skipping a beat, Cil carries on with what she was saying to Bree.

No, it wasn't. I was genuinely hoping you would choose to go back to rehab. I wanted you to save yourself.

Anyway.

She stands.

I am going to honour all the things you asked for. And I've added a couple more perks. The tire voucher on Terry's truck is upgraded to the really fat ones, and I'll give you some vintage New England Patriots merch from back in the day. Old time's sake.

> *She pushes the red send button. We hear a MIGHTY RUSH OF WATER and a WHOOSHING SOUND.*

Bye Bree.

END

Defence of Kayowa wa Bayombo

Tchitala Nyota Kamba

translated by Susan Ouriou

ARTIST'S STATEMENT

From a very young age, I was fascinated by my mother's tales of the life of the beautiful Kayowa wa Bayombo, the Luba woman said to have brought ruin down on the Bakwa-Dishi clans (the clan to which I belong) centuries ago by causing a fratricidal war that led to countless lives being lost. Years later, I decided to immortalize this character – one among many of the grand female figures who have marked the history of the Luba of Kasaï – who did, in fact, exist but whose lifestory has taken on mythic proportions. My decision was part of my desire to reflect some of the elements that have forged my Congolese identity and to denounce the injustice and violence suffered by the women of yesterday and today both in my country of birth and in my adopted home of Canada.

Under the spell of the power of Kayowa's story, I began writing this truly Congolese tale in French in the form of a play, "La Défense de Kayowa wa Bayombo" as a denunciation of the unjust proceedings that led to her execution and a calling-out of the true culprit, her rapist Mubikayi wa Kapumbe. As a playwright, I could envisage her great beauty, the tableaux formed by the many intrigues that marked her life, the places and dress of the time, and hear in my mind again the heroic and ancient Luba chant, the "Kasàlà Chant," that opened a door into my imagination, the first step in bringing her story to the stage.

My desire to see Kayowa's story on a stage was aided by the memory of my late brother Muntu Bidingija, who always had such confidence in me. I am also so grateful for the invitation to board this pirogue as one of seven wonderful women willing to trust in a common vision and explore unknown horizons. It has been both a healing and a creative journey. Our pirogue will soon reach its destination, thanks, in part, to the calm, steady hand of Suzanne, Linda and Cheryl as they guided us on our journey.

CHARACTERS

*(some could be played by the same actor,
some voices in voiceover)*

Kayowa wa Bayombo

Orator

Chief Mutombo Katshi

Voices of the Crowd

Lawyer 1

Lawyer 2

SETTING

Modern courtroom

A soft spotlight comes up on a striking African statue on stage. The actors can either be scattered around the stage or can enter separately to present their argument then sit in an assigned spot.

ORATOR: In the Bayombo clan, Kayowa succumbed to the tragic fate reserved for beautiful mystics such as Kapinga wa Tshiyamba, Kabedi wa ba Ndiadia and many more.

Yo, yo, yoooooo, yo, yo, yo, yoyoooo!

Yo, yo yo, yo, yo yoyoyo, yooooooo!

Kayowa was beautiful.

Her lithe form, delicately sculpted by the Creator, was like the body of the goddesses who only appear in dreams. Her cinammon-coloured skin was sprinkled with the beauty marks found only among young Bayombo-Bashilele girls. Her wide eyes, shaped like the white-gold shells of Lake Munkamba, gave her the piercing gaze of a divinity from beyond the grave. The cowrie shells round her neck evoked the strength and power of the Ocean itself.

And what to say of her high cheekbones that invited a caress, her full mouth, ivory teeth and devouring lips that begged for a kiss. Her long waves of thick black hair braided in the preferred style of the Kasaï women… her long legs like shapely plantains that contributed to her incomparable charm and grace.

(indignant) How dare we decide the fate of a woman, deny her humanity and abuse her existence here on earth simply because of her exceptional splendour? Kayowa was beautiful. Kayowa wa Bayombo was unique!

CHIEF MUTOMBO KATSHI: You, Kayowa wa Bayombo, were properly wed according to our customs. Whatever led you to leave your home, to set peaceful citizens against each other, sowing death among innocent clan members gone to war over a woman? These acts make you a criminal. Your crime has led to the death sentence. You shall disappear before our very eyes.

LAWYER 1: Your Honour, upon hearing the verdict, all those assembled chanted a traditional Luba refrain condemning crimes and criminals:

CROWD: *Tshibaooo, tshibaooo!* Crime, *ee, oo!* Criminal!

SINGLE VOICE FROM CROWD: And who should the crime devour?

CROWD: The perpetrator Kayowa wa Bayombo!

SINGLE VOICE FROM CROWD: As it has been said, woe be to those who rain scandal down on us!

> The CHIEF, *representing the executioner Muka Kanyinda wa Diulu, has* KAYOWA WA BAYOMBO *climb up to the gallows prepared to hang her from the Nsanga tree.* KAYOWA *asks to speak to those assembled before the hanging.*

KAYOWA WA BAYOMBO: I, Kayowa wa Bayombo, sullied and distressed, find myself here on the gallows beneath the Nsanga tree, condemned unanimously by Chief Mutombo Katshi and his allies from the Bakwa-Dishi clan for a crime I did not commit. Condemned to be hanged here on the same square where I and other women from my village came to market one day. A fateful day for me. I was kidnapped, raped and held hostage by Mubikayi, the son of Chief Kapumbe of the Bakwa Tshimuna clan.

Deprived of the right to speak in my defence, I will be
hanged. My grief-stricken heart will accompany me
and the child growing inside me to the grave and to the
Afterlife. Despite my pleas, no Bakwa-Dishi wise man
has seen fit to believe in my innocence. Neither have
the women from my own village! Not a single soul has
defended me.

Lights go down on KAYOWA who continues to witness the rest
of the scene but as a specter.

LAWYER 1: Today, Your Honour, we evoke an event that took
place centuries ago before the colonizers arrived among
the Bakwa-Dishi clans. The event we refer to is that of
a woman's hanging, but not just any woman. A woman
known for her sublime beauty. Since the day of Kayowa's
execution, happiness eludes many young Bakwa-Dishi
girls once they marry. Over the years, brides end up true
victims of physical and verbal abuse within their couple.
Despite the teachings to respect marital customs.

Beaten by their spouses, some die, others are humiliated
and abandoned and become nothing more than baby-
making machines. One fine morning, they find themselves
on the street like stray dogs. And yet all were properly
married according to their clans' customs. There are
numerous examples.

During the following speech, LAWYER 2 could hold up a
photocopy of victims' pictures.

Here we have the case of Mangabu, treated like an object
by her husband. One day, he threw a stool at her head,
provoking her death.

LAWYER 2 lays the picture down on a table, a chair or the floor.

Another case is that of Musawu (*LAWYER 2 holds up another picture*), who, seven months pregnant, was thrown down the stairs by her drunken spouse. The shock was so great she immediately gave birth to her baby, stillborn.

Lays down this picture as well.

These are Bakwa-Dishi women and there are many more cases. All are troubling and Bakwa-Dishi families live in torment asking themselves, why so much misfortune, why so many failed marriages and so much abuse of their daughters?

KAYOWA: (*emerging from the shadows*) Those who judged me believed blame could only lie with the woman kidnapped, raped and murdered, never with the man responsible for the kidnapping, rape and murder. A belief so all-pervasive that even I, in that time and that place, was blinded by it. So much so that my last words on the gallows were these: The Bakwa-Dishi elders have accepted neither my pleas nor my innocence. And so, this is my last request: That in the entire Bakwa-Dishi land, no woman ever be pardoned for similar acts. That she be subjected to death just as I am now.

Beat.

Thus, the injustices have continued for centuries. In my land and elsewhere.

LAWYER 2: Your Honour, Kayowa's case in the past and the cases of Bakwa-Dishi women today are an issue of conscience, not unlike what we have seen in Canada with the tragedy of missing and murdered Indigenous women and girls, kidnapped, raped, and murdered. We have all heard the stories (*LAWYER 1 could hold up and lay down several pictures*) from the Highway of Tears, the infamous farm in Port Coquitlam, along the roads and deep in the woods of every province and territory, the tragic fate of our sisters forever burned into our collective conscience.

A list so long and, as with Kayowa, cases in which justice has never been served.

LAWYER 1: Growing up in Africa, my dreams often turned to the country that I'd learned about in school, Canada, the beautiful, vast, harmonious country with such admirable human rights and equality for women. Yet that was only a mirage. The minute I stepped off the plane at Montreal's Mirabel airport, wide-eyed, my only desire was to see, touch and know the First Peoples I'd heard about in my social studies classes, the ones who had populated my dreams ever since. However, to my great disappointment, I saw no First Nations upon my arrival. I scanned the crowds in vain. And so, I made it my mission to ask questions. I heard of the standoff in Kanehsata:ke, the attempt by successive governments to "kill the Indian in the child." I learned of the broken treaties signed with the First Peoples and of the tragedy of missing and murdered Indigenous women and girls. These young girls and women from the First Peoples of a country, this country, held up by so many as a land where human rights reign, a country dreamed of by others, Canada.

LAWYER 2: Why such inequity and contempt for women and such a tragic fate? And on this their own land. Simply because they were Indigenous and beautiful, a living reminder of the injustices visited on their peoples in the present and past.

Before the time of the colonizers, Indigenous women played an important role as equals or matriarchs within their own societies. The fur traders, when they arrived, in large part survived thanks to the assistance they received from Indigenous women, whom some married "à la façon du pays." But as the eighteenth century neared, racism and sexism reared its fearsome head in the stolen land. And injustice prevailed.

LAWYER 1: Just as it had at the time of Kayowa's hanging, when no one stood up for that woman of the distant past.

We are here to stand up for Kayowa today, for every Disho woman who has lost her life, for every Indigenous women who has lost hers. Centuries late, but we are here, now, for them all, to speak the truth, to right the wrongs, to foster reconciliation.

KAYOWA: (*stepping out from the shadows*) At last, voices raised on my behalf! And on behalf of all those other women wrongly accused, all those mistreated, abused, left for dead. Justice at last to be served.

LAWYER 2: Whether in Canada, Africa or elsewhere, we must ensure respect and honour for all those who have been wronged.

ORATOR: May justice be served! In the case of Kayowa wa Bayombo and for every other woman to whom justice has been denied.

KAYOWA: Justice for us all. For we women are the grand-mothers, the mothers and the daughters of our lands.

> *KAYOWA walks off stage as she chants the song "Kasàlà." She could carefully pick up each photo, first of the Bakwa-Dishi women, then of the missing and murdered Indigenous women and girls, and clasp them to her.*

KAYOWA: Yo, yo, yoooooo, yo, yo, yo, yoyoooo! Yo, yo yo, yo, yo yoyoyo, yooooooo!

> *Lights dim.*

END

The Sacred/Wakân

Porcupine Woman
(Sherry Letendre)

ARTIST'S STATEMENT

In writing my scene for the Many Mothers project, I envisioned a Nakota woman, wrapped in a blanket, travelling throughout the four stages of life within the colours of the medicine wheel. During her journey, she encounters the trauma caused by colonization and emerges on the other side into a space of cultural and spiritual healing and reawakening. It was important for me to create a strong voice. When I write "THEY defined us," "THEY talked about us" and "THEIR word 'Indian,'" it is to underline how racism and white privilege have affected us in our lives. I believe the scenes we, the collective, have written are a way to begin a dialogue of reconciliation in our communities and to empower our youth.

In my language, the word *Nakota* means "an alliance of friends." I was unsure at first whether I had my place in the Many Mothers collective since the other members already worked in the artistic space while the things I talk about are lived experiences. But the moments of sharing with these women were powerful and I came to see them as both allies and friends. I was also deeply touched when the actors read our scripts, especially when one young Indigenous actor became emotional during my scene and our talk about the children sent to residential schools whose unmarked graves had just been found. Those children chose to reveal themselves from the other side at this time for a reason. We must be present to listen and to act.

Girl, school girl, young woman, mature woman
*(all could be played by one actor only or each character
could be played by a different actor)*

Singer/drummer

SETTING
Either four blankets on the ground in a big circle, one yellow, one red, one black, one white, marking the four directions, or a large tipi into which the woman crawls and re-exits (or a new actor emerges) for each new stage with a new blanket. The young woman starts upstage. In the centre (or off to stage left or right), a singer/drummer. On the back wall, a projection of the medicine wheel showing the same colors.

The four different stages of one Nakota woman's life are represented by the colours while the actor on stage lives out those stages and the drummer drums four times to signal each new stage, softly through the narration describing the direction, then stops.

SCENE I

A spotlight shines on the yellow blanket, which lifts up as the girl comes out from underneath and begins to mimic movements to represent a curious child, including a dance. The child will dance and perform while telling the story.

GIRL: (*who dances, twirls, smiles as she speaks during this first part*)

Yellow represents the East, a new beginning and rejuvenation,
where the sun rises,
for new life,
for childhood,
and the direction my Nakota people came from.

As a child, I remember feeling free,
exploring the world around me without fear,
walking through the forest to find berries,
listening to the birds as they talked to each other,
running barefoot in the mud on rainy days,
getting lost in the tall grass and looking to the skies,
wondering what was beyond those clouds,
wondering where we went after we died,
wondering if that was where Creator lived.
Then one day, I went to live with my grandparents to learn
   how to be a good Nakota relative.

Here she wraps the blanket around her waist to show the transition from a dancing child to a young child learning to work and help her grandparents.

Every morning, it was always the same routine,
rise with the sun,
eat breakfast,
do chores.
Every Saturday, grandfather got the horse and wagon ready
while grandmother packed the grub box with food before
   we left for the day-long trip
to the store three miles away.
At the store, grandmother always bought treats for us.
Like nice juicy oranges,
or the bubbly orange crush pop,
or the white peppermint candies.
Mmmm, my favorites.
But we had to wait till after lunch to have any treats.
On the way home, grandfather always stopped at the same
   place in the forest
to rest and feed the horses.
Then he would make a fire so grandmother could cook.
This one time while I was watching, grandfather said,
   (*uses deep voice*) "Granddaughter, go borrow some dishes
   from Magoshin" (*pronounced Ma-goo-sheen*).
I looked all around wondering where this other grandmother lived because there were no houses in sight.
And before I could go anywhere,
he chuckled,
took my hand and walked me over to a willow bush and
   explained,
(*same deep voice*) "Everything (*waving arm left-right*) is loaned
   to us by Creator to use. We can't be wasteful and just go
   around cutting trees for no reason. Everything in nature
   is alive, they are our relatives too." Then he broke off
   the ends of two willow branches, the very leafiest part,

and showed me how to put one on top of the other to make
a plate. And that is how we ate on plates that grandmother
loaned us.

*She picks up the two branches and hugs herself. There will be
no more dancing.*

That was my childhood in my Nakota family,
feeling loved and belonging,
feeling safe.
Then one day I had to go to school…

She puts down the willow branches and picks up a tattered book.

SCENE II

*Spotlight dims and the young girl either runs to the next blanket,
the red one, or crawls into the tipi and out again. The spotlight
then comes up on the red blanket.*

SCHOOLGIRL: Red represents the North where the four-legged
  relatives are,
It represents hardship and danger,
It is for the end of childhood, and the beginning of the
  school years,
and for a time when my Nakota spirit faded into the pages
  of their books.
My father died,
And I started Indian Day School.
A cold place,
A place of displacement,

of becoming invisible,
of losing my voice,
of losing my identity.
And through settler eyes,
THEY defined us,
THEY talked about us,
yet THEY didn't talk about us.
And while at THEIR school,
I learned their reading, 'riting, 'rithmetic,
and THEIR word "Indian."
THEY said,
Indians were welfare people,
Indians were lazy,
Indians were drunks,
Indian women were squaws.
THEY said that!
   (*points outward*)
And nobody ever asked us to tell the real story,
   (*points to herself*)
the story from the People of THIS Land.
   (*points down to the ground*)
From that cold place, I was bullied and abused.
And slipped into a long period of being lost in darkness.

> *With the following line, she slowly sinks to the floor, her arms*
> *wrapped around her body.*

Days turned into weeks,
weeks into years
and piece by piece, I withered.

SCENE III

Spotlight dims and the schoolgirl crawls to the black blanket
or into the tipi and back out and shields her eyes to look for
something in the distance.

YOUNG WOMAN: Black represents the West,
where the thunders and water keepers are,
where the healing water comes from.
The same healing waters that kept me strong during the dark
  years of adulthood.
The period of time when I walked in darkness,
searching for light,
for meaning,
for purpose,
for belonging.

The young woman slowly rises and turns to each direction for
each prayer, arms raised as though giving an offering of tobacco.

I prayed and asked Waka for guidance with my education,
  but I didn't find myself there,
I prayed and asked Waka for guidance in my relationships,
  but I didn't find myself there,
I prayed and asked Waka for guidance with my children,
  but I didn't find myself there,
I prayed and asked Waka for guidance with my church studies,
  but I didn't find myself there,
Then I prayed with my eagle feather and raised it up to the
  skies to Waka *(raises eagle feather)*
and asked for help to find myself,
buried it and waited...

Eventually, I resorted to their firewater to calm the storm
within me,

> *During the following words, the young woman clutches herself
> and sinks to the ground again.*

Battling thoughts of
Suicide,
Addiction,
Abuse,
Violence,
Depression,
Fear,
Loneliness,
Anger,
Self-pity,
Panic attacks that brought me into an abyss,
where I walked through "the valley of the shadow of death."

Then one day, I heard a voice.

VOICE FROM OFFSTAGE: "Wiya, Wiya" (*pronounced Wee-ya, means
woman*)

> *The young woman looks around for the voice calling to her.*

"Gigda" (*pronounced geg da, means get up*)

> *The young woman gets up.*

SCENE IV

Spotlight dims as the woman either moves to the last blanket or into the tipi and out to the white blanket.

MATURE WOMAN: White represents the South where the
winged birds are,
where healing comes from,
it stands for the renewal of life,
and the time when I found my way back to my spirit.

In 1999, I returned back to my Nakota ceremonies to reclaim
my spirit.
Through the sweat lodge,
I experienced cleansing and release from the grip of
addiction.
Through the Sundance lodge,
I found the courage to make new vows and reconcile with
my womanhood.

The mature woman walks to the East and picks up the willow plate, then to the North and picks up the tattered book.

Through living Nakota kinship every day, I found the
strength to repair my broken relationships.

The mature woman turns to the West and picks up the eagle feather.

During the final lines below, the mature woman places the willow plate, the book and the eagle feather on the white blanket as in an offering to the act of healing.

Through prayer,
through compassion,
through helping others,
I live now to honour and heal Mother Earth.

> *Drummer begins to sing and drum the Grandmother's song by Heston Letendre, "You've always been there for me/Here I am singing for you" — either short or long version — as lights dim.*

END

Long Shadows/ kino potasin

Karen W. Olson

In a time when the world began to isolate, seven women came together as Many Mothers to collaborate and create a set of dramatic scenes arising from our thoughts of the dreams, visions and hopes we had for the girls, women and mothers in this world. In conversations, a thread that flowed among the words was our concern and care for this world. Being born and raised on a Manitoba reserve, I had daily access to wondrous gifts from Mother Earth. I spent the summer mostly barefoot, and in winter I lived to skate on the river or slide down the banks, crowded with the neighbours' kids onto broken car hoods. Being outside, being in the bush was natural. When I look back at my growth from childhood to womanhood, I see that it was my mother who guided my way to understanding what was actually in the bush. Medicines. Food. Art supplies. Knowledge.

My mother was Wawaskesiw iskwe, Little Elk Woman. She entered the Midewewin Lodge of the Western Doorway in her 50s and rose to achieve a Fourth Degree recognition. While born a Muskaigo nehiwiyan, she learned the songs, stories and healing ways of the Anishinaabe, and would regularly smoke her pipe to pray for the people. She built a sweat lodge in her yard and hung ribbons and made food offerings in the bush around the house. And then she changed. My mother was swallowed by Alzheimer's. Over the years, the family watched helplessly as our vibrant mother and grandmother began to shrink in mind, body and spirit. Her memories moved into a place she could no longer access. When she left this world, her lodge family said beautiful prayers, told beautiful stories, and to the sound of little boy water drums, they sang for their beloved sister, auntie and grandmother Omashkoons ikwe iban, and honoured her life.

The scene "Long Shadows/kino potasin" is a story of memory and motherhood. Mother Earth provided my mother with vast knowledge. As this knowledge began to fade and fall into the shadows of her memories, my mother's place in my life shifted. As her daughter, it was my turn to nurture her, to dress her, to feed her and to humour her out of a bad mood. My sisters and our families did what we could to make her comfortable and loved. As I wrote this scene, I shed tears. I mourned for the times I would never have with my mother. I mourned for the sound of her laughter and being teased by gentle humour. I mourned for the stories and the songs that she would never share again. When those tears dried, my fingers flew over the keys as my memories, my stories flooded in.

In gratitude to the six women I wrote with and worked alongside, I put seven coloured ribbons around a birch tree in the bush behind my mother's house in Peguis. In honour and respect to Nikawiy (my mother), I draped a string of twenty-one tobacco ties beside the ribbons. These offerings will be changed by the wind, the rain and the snow. In time, they will fade and fall to the ground. Mother Earth will accept these with endless love and grace.

CHARACTERS
Nitanis (Daughter)
Nikawiy (Mother)
Nikokum (Grandmother)

SETTING
Outdoors

Dark stage, a single light shines on a figure upstage. NIKOKUM sits in a chair facing west, drumming softly.

NIKAWIY enters, walks toward a chair placed centre stage with a shawl draped over the back. She settles into her chair, puts the shawl on her lap and looks around at those gathered, smiling and nodding at some.

NIKAWIY begins to talk. A Storyteller, she moves with her story.

NIKAWIY: The word to greet people in my language is Tansi. It's an easy word to learn. Two syllables. Just like Hello. Hel Loh. Tansi. Tan Si.

NIKAWIY adjusts the shawl, and looks at the audience.

Tansi.

NIKAWIY pauses.

Nikokum was always telling stories of the past. She made it sound as if all the people did was have fun all the time. I used to regret that I wasn't alive in her time. I don't think that way anymore. I know the other stories now. The sad stories. The horror stories that she did not tell. Those stories that are being told now. To me. To you. To the world. The stories that break our hearts.

NIKAWIY pauses.

Our people still have fun. We smile and we laugh. And we chase the memory of those other stories away. Never far. Just away. And only for a while.

NIKAWIY smiles and shakes her head.

NIKOKUM drums louder, does check beats. NIKOKUM stands and dances downstage to left stage of NIKAWIY.

NIKAWIY: We dance to settler music. Yeah, we rock out, we jazz it up, ballet it up too. But we started with the jig. Those settlers brought the fiddle and we loved it.

NIKAWIY hums a fiddle tune and moves her feet in jigging motions.

But the best… oh, the absolute best is when we dance to our own music. The big drum at pow wows. The hand drum at round dances. The water drum in the Lodge. We sing in our own language too!

NIKOKUM sings softly in Cree.

NIKAWIY: My language was once called a sin. Our words evil. Our dances evil.

In the background, projected still or video images of dancers performing a round dance. NIKOKUM begins to drum a round dance beat.

NIKAWIY stands, removes and drapes the shawl over her arm, then moves downstage to bounce in place to the rhythm of the drum beat. She slowly dances a round dance step while facing the audience.

NIKOKUM does a loud beat and stops.

NIKAWIY stops dancing. Background projection also stops.

NIKAWIY: The nimiwin was in the arbour. We danced fast. We danced slowly. We danced in the sunlight. We danced in the moonlight. We danced in a circle.

NIKOKUM softly drums a straight pow wow beat as NIKAWIY steps forward into the graceful dance steps of a women's traditional dancer. Image projected of dancers in a semi-circle and dancing in place.

NIKAWIY: I dance today with the wind. My bones a drumstick. My heart a drum. I sing to the earth, to askiy, with soft breath.

NIKAWIY dances and turns a full circle.

Nimiwin! Nimiwin! I dance upon the grass with MY music in my heart… with MY words in my mouth… with pride in MY spirit.

NIKAWIY dances off stage.

NITANIS enters and assists NIKOKUM to sit in the chair at centre. NITANIS removes four long ribbons — red, green, yellow, black — from a pocket and lays them across the old lady's lap. NIKOKUM pats her arm and they look lovingly at one another.

Background shows a starry night sky with a moon.

NITANIS: Nikokum always told stories of the past.

NIKOKUM: Turn your eyes to the night sky. Nikomis, Grandmother Moon, sits on a blanket of stars. Look, my girl. She is cradled in perfect balance.

NITANIS: She spirals toward a fading night… she moves our world toward a new beginning. Every night, she does her work. I see her. I feel her. I know her.

NIKOKUM: Across the miles, across sacred land, across generations. We live. We breathe. Each day, time passes in sacred existence.

NITANIS/NIKOKUM: (*the women speak together*) We live each day remembering.

NIKOKUM and NITANIS pause to smile lovingly at one another.

NITANIS: Ayyyyyy, you memorized my poem.

NIKOKUM: Eyhey. I like how you tell those poems… those word stories. Did I ever tell you the story of how our Grandmother Moon came to be?

NITANIS: Tell me again. It's been long since you told me a story.

NIKOKUM: This is a story I heard from my friend Eleanor Brass from Peepeekis. Once, there was this spirit helper who looked after the sun. With his son and daughter, they lived together in the sky. Their father was always busy keeping the great fire of the sun burning. He was away all day and only came home at night.

NITANIS: Just like Notawiy. Dad worked all day too.

NIKOKUM nods.

NIKOKUM: Ehey. One day, the father felt the weariness of old age and spoke to his children. They were adults now. "My son and daughter, you know that I'm getting old. I cannot tend to the sun's fire much longer. I'll be leaving you soon and it will be up to one of you to keep the fire burning. If you let it go out, the people and animals will die."

NITANIS: That's a big job eh?

NIKOKUM nods.

NIKOKUM: Ehey. The children loved their father and said they would not let him down. Then one day, their father died. The children mourned through the night and when morning came, they argued over who would tend the fire. The girl, who was getting tired of taking care of the tipi and doing all the cooking and cleaning, thought she should do it.

NITANIS: (*loudly*) I am the oldest. I should tend the fire.

NIKOKUM: The boy thought differently. As boys and girls tend to do.

NITANIS: (*in a gruff voice*) I am the protector of the camp. I should tend the fire.

NIKOKUM: Oh, those two they argued all morning. Meanwhile down here on Earth, the humans and animals were getting worried. The sun was not as bright as it always had been.

NITANIS cries out mournfully.

NITANIS: Why is it so cold? What happened to the sun?

NIKOKUM: Well, Old Wesakachak got worried. It was getting dark during the day and colder. So away he went to the sky. He saw the brother and sister arguing. Oh boy, he got mad!

NIKOKUM points her lips toward audience member.

NIKOKUM: You, being the man, it will be up to you to keep the fire of the sun burning during the day. Your name is pisim.

NITANIS: The sun.

NIKOKUM's lip points in another direction.

NIKOKUM: And you, young woman. Since you are so anxious to keep a fire burning, you too will keep a fire, but yours will never have flames and will only shine at night. You will have to work hard to keep the coals glowing and never let them go out. Your name is tipiskawe pisim.

NITANIS: Night Sun. The moon.

NIKOKUM: And then old Wesakachak takes it farther. "Because you couldn't get along and nearly destroyed the Earth, you will only be with one another once a year. For the rest of the time, you will only look at one another from across the sky."

NITANIS: The annular solar eclipse. That's what they call it now. That's when tipiskawe pisim crosses over and casts a shadow over her brother pisim. It is such a sacred time for them that we are not even allowed to look at it. They will see each other soon.

NIKOKUM: I'm getting tired, my girl. You know the story. Keep telling it. Keep remembering.

NIKOKUM rises.

Say the rest of your poem. I love to hear your words, my girl.

NITANIS: Many generations have lived upon these sacred lands. They breathed clean air. Generations of our children will breathe this same air. They will live upon these sacred lands.

NITANIS rises, she and NIKOKUM hold hands and look at each other.

NITANIS/NIKOKUM: (*the women speak together*) Across many miles, across sacred lands, across generations, we live and breathe each day. As time passes in sacred existence, we live each day remembering.

NIKOKUM is drumming softly as she returns to the chair.

NITANIS: Remember. Remember. Remember.

NITANIS pauses a moment, then looks around at the audience.

NITANIS: My mother is changing. Nikawiy is different. Shadows grow deep inside her mind. Long shadows that pull and strip away her knowledge, making cuts into her memories.

Sounds of nature in background… birds, tree leaves moving, water.

Meanwhile, time has passed. An older NIKAWIY enters wearing an old sweater inside out. She goes to NIKOKUM who hands her three ribbons — red, yellow, green. NIKAWIY moves to stage left, raises her hands as if to stroke leaves.

NIKAWIY: I knew the name of this tree. Waskwoyahtik! It's a birch tree. I knew this medicine. Once, I sat in the cool shade of these branches to prepare tobacco ties for the lodge.

NIKAWIY lets the green ribbon slip through her fingers and moves to centre stage, touches the ground.

I knew places where the medicine plants grow… neta, wapikwaniya. Over there, those flowers. I knew their medicine. Once, I sat in sunlit meadows filled with those same flowers to braid sweetgrass for the lodge.

Twenty-one strands. Seven for the past, seven for the present, seven for the future.

> *NIKAWIY lets the yellow ribbon slip through her fingers and moves to stage right.*

I knew the depth of roots… neta, wihkas. Over there, muskrat root. I knew that medicine. Once, I dropped so deep into the bog my foot got stuck. Got stuck so good my boot got pulled off. Oh my, that was hard crawling out of there, me laughing, everyone laughing. Darn Ol' Kathy not even helping. Wah! And you…

> *NIKAWIY is laughing as she lets the final ribbon slip through her fingers and walks empty-handed toward NITANIS, pointing and smiling.*

NIKAWIY: You were no help at all. Laughing at your mom like that.

> *NITANIS laughs. She takes NIKAWIY by the hand.*

NITANIS: Not that time, Nikawiy. Not that time.

> *NITANIS goes to the green ribbon and picks it up.*

You KNOW the songs.

NIKAWIY: Kekwan ihtwewina? What are the words?

> *NITANIS comforts NIKAWIY.*

NITANIS: I know the words… I know the songs.

> *NITANIS picks up the yellow ribbon.*

You KNOW the dances.

NIKAWIY: Tantahto-aya? What are the steps?

NITANIS comforts NIKAWIY.

NITANIS: I know the steps. I know the dances.

NITANIS picks up the red ribbon.

You KNOW the stories. Nikawiy, you know the stories that the stones tell.

NIKAWIY: Taniwa? Where? Taniwa asinyak? Where are the stones?

NITANIS comforts NIKAWIY. They walk toward NIKOKUM.

NITANIS: I know where those stones are. Someday, I will hear their stories. Someday, I might even tell their stories.

NITANIS takes the black ribbon from her pocket and lays it across the floor a few feet in front of NIKOKUM's feet. She and NIKAWIY each stand at her side and lay a hand on her shoulder.

NIKOKUM stands, turns to look at NIKAWIY and puts the shawl over NIKAWIY's shoulders. NIKOKUM takes a step and then turns to look back at NITANIS and gives her the drum. NITANIS plays the drum.

NIKOKUM turns forward, crosses over the black ribbon and downstage, singing strongly, steps down from the stage and walks into the audience.

END

Signs

Susan Ouriou

ARTIST'S STATEMENT

This journey began for me with the birth of my first grand-child and the wave of pure joy and sheer terror that washed over me at the stark realization of the fragility of each new life and the precarity of the world my grandson and his generation would inherit. A wave of guilt too, which I knew from my griefwork is but a stand-in for the true emotions underlying it – sadness and anger. I also knew the absolute need to express those emotions if I and we are to find a way forward. "Signs" is my attempt at just that, writing words, music and lyrics that I dreamt of seeing embodied on stage as a way of forging, in real time and real space, a connection with others. A dream that is now being realized. One very small step toward making a difference for our children and grand-children and the seven generations to come.

I am eternally grateful to the other Mothers for the wisdom they bring and have brought through many years of friendship. I give thanks to Joan, Tchitala, Karen, Sherry, Cheryl and Linda for creating a village together out of shared love and laughter and sorrow and hope; to the mentors – Jenna Rodgers, Michelle Thrush, Reneltta Arluk and Denise Clarke; to Oli Siska, for help writing the grants; to the directors and actors who gave of their talents; to Anna Lumière and Christie Simmons for their musical skill (Anna composing the music for "One Cosmos" and Christie writing the song "Nathan"); to Barbara Joan Scott for seeing the whole; to

Kelsey Attard and Freehand Books for the gift of publishing this anthology; to Brian Quirt and Daniel Libman for sharing their knowledge of theatre; to Bob Pearson, Sarah Edwards, Trevor Matheson, Olek Janusz, Pam Taylor, Katheryn Morrissette, and Dominic Terry of Heritage Park; Kennedy Greene, our production and stage manager, musician Barbara Joan Scott and actors Wakefield Brewster and Christopher Hunt for their willingness to accompany us onto the stage; to my daughter, son-in-law and grandchildren who remind me every day of the importance of ensuring their future; and to my husband, Joël, for tending the home fires. Let us together make the impossible possible.

CHARACTERS
Suzanne, writer, sister to Dan, mother to Katie
Barbara, guitarist/singer
Bird, recording

To listen to recordings of the songs in "Signs," visit: **https:// soundcloud.com/search?q=rowboat%20susan%20ouriou** and click on the arrow next to the song you would like to hear. (Lyrics and music for "Run Nathan Run" by Christie Simmons based on the novel *Nathan* by Susan Ouriou; lyrics and music for "Rowboat" and "Humankind" by Susan Ouriou; "One Cosmos" lyrics by Susan Ouriou, music by Anna Lumière. On the recordings, "Run Nathan Run" is performed by Christie Simmons and "Rowboat," "Humankind" and "One Cosmos" are performed by Barbara Joan Scott.)

SETTING
A workshop

Stage right is a stool next to a long table piled high with poster boards, wooden stakes, felt pens, a newspaper, a worn blanket, a binder, a Frisbee, a popcorn pail, a scribbler, a bird's nest and a staple gun. Another stool is set up stage left with a guitar stand beside it and a window. There is a projection screen upstage. During her monologue, when SUZANNE switches into and out of the present, a spotlight could be used. As the lights come up, SUZANNE makes her way to centre stage with other poster stakes under her arm while BARBARA, her guitar slung over her shoulder, walks to the stool stage left. SUZANNE smiles looking out at the audience.

SUZANNE: *(to audience)* Look at all the volunteers come to help us make signs today.

SUZANNE heads toward the table, calling back over her shoulder.

Don't worry, I won't really put you to work. In fact, my friend Barbara and I have got a few songs to share with you to help pass the time.

SUZANNE nods at BARBARA, who strums a few chords. At the table, SUZANNE lays down the stakes, picks up a felt pen, pulls a poster board up close, sits on the stool and bends over to write on the board.

It would be great though to be able to count on you in our cause. We're planning a march. The least we can do for our children. And with our children. Show our young people we'll not let their future be robbed.

BARBARA stops strumming, SUZANNE looks up.

Two of the youth in my life had that future stolen.

SUZANNE glances back at the screen where a picture goes up of a young Dan.

Dan, my little brother. A cute, curious, quiet kid, (*waving felt pen*) always drawing pictures and reading dinosaur books. Who grew up to study architecture and win an award for the survival hut he designed.

Beat.

Shouldn't that mean you would have survived, little brother?

Picture of Dan at 20 goes up.

Home from university that last summer, Dan and his friends drive to the Rockies, pitch their tents above Toby Creek.

A picture of the landscape above Toby Creek goes up.
SUZANNE glances at the screen.

They grab a Frisbee. But the game ends when the Frisbee cracks. And it's Dan who offers to send the broken Frisbee off the nearby cliff. He didn't know then what I learned later.

SUZANNE rummages through the objects on the table to find the newspaper and reads out loud.

Researchers have found that young males have a false sense of invincibility. Their brains are still developing, trying to catch up to their bodies. For that reason, they tend to have an unnaturally high accident and mortality rate.

SUZANNE lays down the paper.

So it's Dan, thinking he's invincible, who steps up to the edge of the cliff.

SUZANNE stands, picks up the Frisbee and draws close to the edge of the stage.

But an outcrop lower down blocks the view to the creek sixty metres below. It would be so much better to throw the Frisbee from there!

SUZANNE takes a tentative step forward when suddenly her foot slips and we hear the rumbling of falling scree as SUZANNE staggers and tries to catch her balance. Lights and slide off.

Lights slowly come up on SUZANNE with the broken Frisbee clasped to her chest.

Years later, I go to see for myself that cliff, that drop. Stand where Dan stood. Feel the wind, feel the sun. Look up above.

Slide of a raven in a blue sky behind her on the screen.

A raven soared overhead. Soon to be joined by another. The two danced together against the blue of the sky, wheeling and gliding from one current to the next.

Then I remembered. My brother at five, saying,

Beat.

"When I grow up, I'm going to be a bird."

Lights dim then slowly brighten as SUZANNE returns the Frisbee to the table, and staples her finished sign to a stake. She stands it up against the downstage side of the table where the audience sees the following message — "Rob No Child of Their Future." She shouts out to the wings.

Ben, your sign's ready!

SUZANNE begins work on the next sign.

I wrote a novel for my brother. Unlike Dan, Nathan, the character in my novel, doesn't die. But he does, for a time, lose the ability to stand, to walk, to run.

> BARBARA *begins strumming intro chords from the last line of the first verse of "Run Nathan Run," then sings while* SUZANNE *continues printing the next sign.*

BARBARA:

Run Nathan run
Oh, run Nathan run
Feel the wind feel the sun
Feel the earth that's under your feet
Run Nathan run
Like you can't be undone
Claim your victory not your defeat
Oh, your victory not your defeat

> SUZANNE *hits the stapler as she nails another poster board to a stake.*

SUZANNE: "Like you can't be undone." That's us, grown-ups today. Acting like we – and more importantly our children – cannot be undone. Thinking we're invincible as though we're the ones with half-developed brains, risking the health of our planet, and endangering our children in the process. When we, the adults in their lives, should be doing everything we can to make the world a safe one for them to grow up in.

> *Picture of young Katie goes up on screen. Catching sight of it,* SUZANNE *speaks almost under her breath.*

The tragedy is, there are times when no one can do anything at all.

Katie. Our youngest daughter.

That trip to emergency for a diagnosis no sixteen-year-old girl, no parent, no sister should ever have to hear. They whisk our daughter away. We sit alone. All alone. Until the doctor appears and takes a seat by my side.

(*SUZANNE adopts doctor's voice*) "I'm here… (*clearing of throat*)… hemorrhaging… in your daughter's brain… We've had to induce a coma."

The doctor stops speaking. For so long. Till I say, unbelieving: "Is she… is she going to die?" (*assuming doctor's voice again*) "I'm so sorry. It's… it's a very rare form of leukemia. That kills within days."

> *Lights go out then up on SUZANNE who picks up a worn blanket while the blanket slide goes up on the screen.*

SUZANNE: Katie and her doudou.

> *SUZANNE rubs the blanket against her cheek.*

The best friend she takes everywhere with her. So loved, so fondled, so laundered that it shrinks by the day, shredding away till it's almost nothing… just a scrap of fabric full of holes.

> *SUZANNE puts down the blanket.*

Katie outgrew her doudou, made friends instead, riding the LRT to the end of the line after school every day to see them off, spending hours on the phone whenever they were apart.

She discovered acting, too, which she loved for those together times, singing scales, rehearsing lines, exploring other lives on-stage and off.

When Katie turned sixteen, our family left for a year's sabbatical in France, her father Joël's home country.

> *Picture of Katie in front of the Eiffel Tower.* SUZANNE *picks up the binder.*

Katie turned to writing the way she'd turned to her doudou as a toddler and to her friends as a young teen. For comfort and to feel that connection. We read those entries and those letters. After.

> SUZANNE *leafs through the binder of Katie's writing.*

Words full of dreams and goals, laughter, encouragement and hope.

In one of the letters, Katie mentioned one goal that was bigger than all the others: "I can't wait to be a mother, despite all the million other things I want to do, I think that will be my favorite."

> *Beat.*

One day our daughter was here, the next she was gone. How can that be?

> SUZANNE *turns to* BARBARA, *who starts playing intro to* "Rowboat" *song.*

In every dream I've had since Katie's last breath, she's been the toddler of so many years ago. But finally, I dreamed of my daughter at sixteen, the age I saw her last, wholly herself. So real. So unreachable. I dreamed a song.

BARBARA sings and plays while SUZANNE strokes the blanket.

BARBARA:
Last night a rowboat waited
On the riverbank for us
I drew near as you turned away
I climbed aboard you waded out

Chorus: If only you would come to me
If only you could
If only you would come to me
If only you could

My rowboat glided gently
Making waves that lapped your side
Cradling the child I bore
The child I was leaving behind

Chorus

I begged you to join me
Somehow knowing all the while
You will wade on and on
Till I too leave the rowboat behind

Chorus

After BARBARA plays the last chord, a BIRD sings and SUZANNE steps over to the window.

SUZANNE: Early every morning those first months after Katie died, a chickadee sang outside my window. Gave me the courage to get up, out of bed. Then, one morning, at the usual hour, there was no chickadee and I could do nothing but sob. Till the tiny bird sang again, giving me a reason to go on…

SUZANNE returns to the table, calling out to the wings.

Amélie, Adama, Archie, your signs are ready.

SUZANNE puts the signs on top of Ben's, one by one, so the audience sees each message before it is covered up, the messages the same as in the slide of the children marching that will go up shortly. SUZANNE turns to the audience.

As true as it is that some children die tragically, like Dan or like Katie, and nothing can be done, I can't help myself from thinking about all those other children, those of the past who went missing on land that was rightly theirs, those children of today we can still do something for, whose world we still have a chance to make better, yet we do so little or nothing at all. Where on earth is the kind in humankind!?

SUZANNE begins furiously stapling more posterboards to stakes and, in the slide that goes up on the screen, while BARBARA strums angrily, young children of all colours and creeds march bearing placards. Their signs read: Desperate for Change; There is No Planet B; No Nature, No Future; If You Don't Act Like Adults, We Will; A Part or Apart; Know Your Medicine; Gigda/Get Up; Speak Truth to Power; Love is Not a Colour. The projection ends. SUZANNE throws down the staple gun and BARBARA stops strumming.

Where is the kind in creating conditions that send children fleeing from ever-more violent and ever-more frequent fires, hurricanes, earthquakes, floods? Or in standing by as species die?

Spotlight on SUZANNE as she stands and paces the stage. Picture of Katie and Christelle goes up on screen.

From the empty nest that our rented apartment in Paris
has become, not long after Katie's death and after her sister
Christelle's return to Canada to start university, our friends
invite us on a weekend away.

To a cabin, a hike in the mountains. A hike during which all
my eyes can see, all my body can feel is the pull of the drop
below. It takes every last ounce of my strength to return to
the cabin unscathed. To sit myself down. To breathe.

That's when a little bird flits through the open door, tilts its
wings at Katie's father, and explores this new space of ours,
only to fly away through that same opening to the great
outdoors.

Beat.

An opening. The realization that there is, in fact, a "kind"
in humankind and that the man I love, the father of our two
girls, is one such example. And that there are many more.

Picture of Joël with Katie goes up on screen briefly as BARBARA
plays and sings the first verse of "Human Kind" while SUZANNE
goes back to making signs.

BARBARA:
You are the kind in humankind
Who makes up for the wrongs of others
You are the one who rights our course
With a gentle stroke of the paddle
You are the father of firstborn joy
And of Katie in the sky with diamonds
You are my future, my present, my past
A light for our children's children

SUZANNE: Our love, his love, your love, our fight for what's right. To find a new way of being so all children born to us and to Mother Earth may live out their lives. There is no future in searching for the meaning of any loss. The only path forward is to give meaning to it all.

Lights out then up on SUZANNE seated with the pail of popcorn in her hands.

Katie's still alive, the diagnosis mere weeks away. The girls ask the two of us to come with them to a movie in the Latin Quarter. Our sixteen- and eighteen-year-old daughters actually want to see a movie with their parents! (*laughing*) Of course, then I realize – when the girls choose seats five rows ahead of our own – that what they really want is tickets and popcorn paid for by someone else!

Oh well, at least the theatre's almost empty so we can still see our girls up ahead.

SUZANNE sets the popcorn down on the floor and leans in.

The movie is *Phenomenon*: John Travolta starring as a man diagnosed with a brain tumour. Even as it works to kill him, the tumour magnifies his brain's capacity. For as long as he can, he uses his newfound genius to save the lives of others.

After the movie, as the girls make their way back up the aisle past us, I slip my arm through Katie's, who says, "I want to be like that." I laugh and say to my daughter, "You mean a rich and famous movie star?" But no, Katie says,

Beat.

"I want to make a difference in the world."

> *Slide of children marching with their signs goes up on screen,*
> *this time accompanied by adults.* SUZANNE *gets to her feet.*

And she will. They will. We will. Katie, Dan, those of us who care, all of us insisting there has got to be another way. A way that shores up Mother Earth – a sanctuary for all creatures, not the least of these our children still here and those to come.

After Joël and I returned to Canada and to Christelle, without Katie, two robins made their home in our back-yard. Behind the lantern on the deck (*picks up nest*), they built their nest out of dead leaves, fallen twigs and lint from our dryer vent, laid eggs – twice that season – pulled worms from the lawn to feed to their little ones, helped their fledglings take flight, then stayed behind. All of us sharing a home. Their message the same as Dan's raven, as the cabin's feathered visitor, as Katie's chickadee.

> BARBARA *starts strumming intro to "One Cosmos" song.*

That we are all kin. Every child, every adult, every bird, animal, fish and tree alive on this our Mother Earth is related. Put here together to look after one another.

All of us one cosmos.

> *Pictures of children's faces go up one after the other on*
> *the screen while* BARBARA *plays and sings.*

BARBARA:
May birds still have a song to sing
No child be robbed of her future
Not Adama, Ben, Archie, Amélie
Nor any of nature's creatures

Turn their dreams into reality
Give them back their world
Undo the damage of history
See their potential unfurl

Chorus: There is no human versus nature
No inside versus out
No us versus Creator
Only one cosmos cosmos Ohohoh…

Together we march to show we care
Strike a balance again
Foster change in myriad ways
Promise to make amends

Chorus

Bridge: We can't breathe
Love is not a colour
There is no Planet B
Part or apart
Speak truth to power
Truth to power truth to power
Truth

Chorus twice then the first two lines of the chorus one last time.

*SUZANNE takes two signs, one is "Rob No Child of Their Future,"
and walks over to BARBARA, who stands. They hug and SUZANNE
hands BARBARA the "A Part or Apart" sign. They join hands and
face the audience.*

BIRD song, lights go down.

END

Making Many Mothers

Linda Gaboriau

Dramaturgical support can take many shapes and forms. I always prefer to shape my support to fit the needs of the writer. In this case, there were six writers coming to the Many Mothers collective from very diverse backgrounds and whose experience in writing for the stage was also diverse. In bringing us together, Susan suggested a working title for our project: URGENCY. Each member was invited to speak about the pressing issues she felt needed to be addressed, be it from an international, environmental, social, political, individual or local community perspective. At the first meeting of the collective in October 2020, words and themes were shared, written on the whiteboard in no particular order. In the ensuing discussions, it was clear that the women wanted to write with a sense of shared goals and concerns. Would, could, those shared goals take the form of one full-length play co-authored by all the members of the collective?

As the women began to draft preliminary scenes, it became clear to me that the most moving and provocative moments emerged when the writer had intimately experienced the reality of the characters and situations portrayed, when the women gave voice to their personal fears and hopes. Should we embrace the second-wave feminists' slogan: *Personal is political?* Would an attempt to weave those scenes into a single script featuring a more narrowly defined dramatic arc inevitably dilute the power of each individual testimony? I began to see the work being written as a score for a chamber music ensemble. Each instrument would have its moment and contribute to the overall impact of the composition. We discussed the pros and cons of the various shapes our theatre production could take at great length. Empathy and mutual respect infused every conversation. And we finally settled on the structure you are discovering in this book, a series of scenes that, as Joan Crate says in her introduction, stand "shoulder-to-shoulder," underscoring the shared concerns that throb beneath the apparently different cultural and individual perspectives.

Ultimately, the best "dramaturgical support" I could offer was to urge each writer to listen to her inner voice, to her personal guides and demons. I could read and listen attentively to the scenes to help identify the throughlines taking shape and, if my reading of the writer's intentions resonated for her, I could encourage her to further hone or develop the dialogue or moments that expressed those intentions most effectively. Listening to the CBC broadcast of Tomson Highway's 2022 Massey Lectures last fall, I couldn't help but smile when Tomson tells us that in Cree culture, divinity is female. As Sherry Letendre said during one group session, we have a duty to channel our stories as medicine, so we can help promote hope and healing in the world around us. How often do we get to hear women who are not public figures speak out about their painful lives or their divine dreams? That was the opportunity participating in the Many Mothers collective gave me. It was a privilege and I learned much more than I was able to give.

ABOUT THE MANY MOTHERS

JOAN CRATE was born in the Northwest Territories at Sǫǫ̀m-bak'è on Chief Drygeese territory, traditional land of the Yellowknives Dene First Nation. After finding homes in various places, she now lives in Calgary – Mohkinstsis – and the rural Okanagan on the unceded territory of sqilxʷ/syilx (Okanagan) peoples. She writes both poetry and fiction and has won several writing awards over the years, including the Writers' Guild of Alberta Golden Pen Award in 2023 and the W.O. Mitchell City of Calgary Book Award for *Black Apple*, which was also shortlisted for the Frank Hegyi Award. The band U2, of whom she's a big fan, featured her poem "I am a Prophet" on screen in their last Canadian tour. She lost her partner of almost four decades at the beginning of the pandemic. Since then, she has had work appear in five anthologies and on CBC radio. She continues to explore writing in all its forms, visual art and is even dabbling in acting.

CHERYL FOGGO is a multiple award–winning playwright, author and filmmaker, whose work over the last thirty years has focused on the lives of Western Canadians of African descent. Recent works include the release of her NFB feature documentary *John Ware Reclaimed*, available on nfb.ca, as well as the thirtieth anniversary edition of her book *Pourin' Down Rain: A Black Woman Claims Her Place in the Canadian West*. Recent journalism can be found in the *Interrupt/Reframe* issue of *The Fold,* on CBC *Black on the Prairies* and in *Westword Magazine*. In 2021, 2022 and 2023, her plays *Heaven* and *John Ware Reclaimed* have received multiple productions, including at The Citadel in Edmonton, Lunchbox Theatre in Calgary, at the Blyth Theatre Festival and in Ottawa at the National Arts Centre. She recently wrapped shooting of a short film about northern Saskatchewan's Black History, scheduled to premiere in 2023. Cheryl is the recipient of the Lieutenant Governor of Alberta Outstanding Artist Award, the Doug and Lois Mitchell Outstanding Calgary Artist Award and the Arts, Media and Entertainment Award from the Calgary Black Chambers, all in 2021. She is a 2022 inductee into the Alberta Order of Excellence.

LINDA GABORIAU is an award-winning dramaturg and literary translator based in Montreal. Her translations of plays by Quebec's most prominent playwrights have been published and produced across Canada and abroad. Recently published and soon to premiere at Centaur Theatre is her translation of Michel Marc Bouchard's play "Embrasse/Kisses Deep." In her work as a dramaturg, she has directed numerous translation residencies and international exchange projects. She was the founding director of the Banff International Literary Translation Centre, has won the Governor General's Award for Translation three times and is a member of the Order of Canada.

TCHITALA NYOTA KAMBA is a Calgary-based writer, actor, poet, drummer and educator, as well as the founder of Miabiwood Film Production (MFP) Ltd. (formerly Apapi Film & Theatre). Originally from the Democratic Republic of the Congo, she has a PhD in French Studies from the Université de Montréal and has published poetry collections, written for the theatre, most recently for the 2021 Ethnik Festival for the Arts, and acted in and directed performances for Calgary's Alliance Française, among others. Her next book, *Kayowa wa Bayombo,* will be published by France's Éditions Amalthée in 2023.

SHERRY LETENDRE is a Coordinator for the Alexis Nakota Sioux Nation Integrated Youth Hub Project. She is also a Facilitator and Community Researcher and her current work is focused on the Nimi Icinohabi Life Skills program and Healthy Relationship Project for youth, to culturally adapt it for grades 10–12 and for young adults and includes some theatre. She is enrolled in the Bachelor of Native Studies program at the University of Alberta. Her journey and passion led her to pursue a career in child and youth care, bringing her back to her own community after years of educating herself. She credits much of her accomplishments to the Creator and to her mother for instilling a vision for change in her community.

KAREN W. OLSON is nehiyaw/anishinaabe of the Marten Clan and from Peguis First Nation. She is the Department Head of Creative Writing at En'owkin Centre and the author of four children's books. Karen is the Artistic Director and founder of Prairie Thunder Arts, an Indigenous performance company. She is passionate about sharing the stories and teachings of her Indigenous heritages.

SUSAN OURIOU is an award-winning fiction writer and literary translator with an interest in theatre and song-writing. She is a Governor General's Award recipient and was most recently shortlisted for that same award for her translations *The Lover, The Lake* by Eeyou author Virginia Pesemapeo Bordeleau of Quebec in 2021 and *White Resin* by Quebec author Audrée Wilhelmy in 2022. She was also shortlisted for the WGA's Georges Bugnet Prize for the first of her two novels, *Damselfish*. She has edited two anthologies: *Beyond Words: Translating the World* and *Languages of Our Land: Indigenous Poems and Stories from Quebec*. In 2010, she was appointed Chevalier in France's Ordre des Arts et des Lettres.